Presented to ....

....

....

....

....

....

....

ISBN 0-374-35106-6

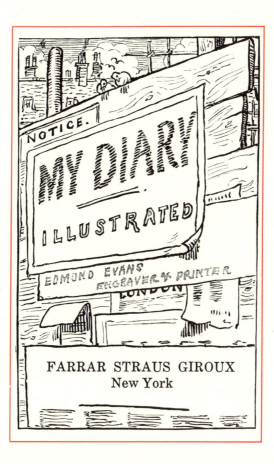

NOTICE.

MY DIARY

ILLUSTRATED

EDMUND EVANS
ENGRAVER & PRINTER
LONDON

FARRAR STRAUS GIROUX
New York

JANUARY 1st.

....

....

....

....

....

New Year's Day.

JANUARY 2nd.

....

....

....

....

Robinson Crusoe caught a
Goat, 1660.

Training ship, "Warspite,"
burnt, 1876.

JANUARY 3rd.

....
....
....
....
....

JANUARY 4th.

....
....
....
....
....

Sandwich Islands discovered, 1778.

JANUARY 5th.

....
....
....
....

Cork Poultry Show, 1870.

Twelfth Night.

JANUARY 6th.

....
....
....
....
....

JANUARY 7th.

....
....
....
....
....

Old Masters at the Royal Academy.

JANUARY 8th.

....
....
....

Skate now, if the ice be fit.

JANUARY 9th.

Experiments with the 38-ton gun, 1879.

JANUARY 10th.

Penny postage commenced, 1840.

JANUARY 11th.

Fox-hunting continues if weather permits.

Sleighing.

JANUARY 12th.

....

....

....

....

JANUARY 13th.

....

....

....

....

Snow man.

Skating meeting on the Fens, 1881.

JANUARY 14th.

....

....

....

....

British Museum opened, 1759.

JANARY 15th.

....

....

....

....

....

JANUARY 16th.

....

....

....

....

....

Dog-days do not commence yet.

JANUARY 17th.

....

....

....

....

Indian Mutiny commenced about
this time, 1857.

Great snow-storm, England, 1881.

JANUARY 18th.

....
....
....
....
....
....

JANUARY 19th.

....
....
....
....
....

More snow.

Defence of Rorke's Drift, 1879.

JANUARY 20th.

....
....
....
....
....

Still Fox-hunting.

JANUARY 21st.

....

....

....

....

....

JANUARY 22nd.

....

....

....

....

....

Chinese Embassy arrived, 1877.

JANUARY 23rd.

....

....

....

....

....

*Lord Salisbury embarked for
England, 1877.*

Great fire, near Bolton, 1877.

JANUARY 24th.

....
....
....
....
....

JANUARY 25th.

....
....
....
....
....

Magic Lantern Nights.

JANUARY 26th.

....
....
....
....

Sliding goes on.

Frozen out.

JANUARY 27th.

....

....

....

....

....

JANUARY 28th.

....

....

....

....

Football.

JANUARY 29th.

....

....

....

....

Robinson Crusoe teaches his Parrot.

Charles I. beheaded, 1649.

JANUARY 30th.

....
....
....
....
....

JANUARY 31st.

....
....
....
....
....

Partridge and Pheasant shooting
ends.

FEBRUARY 1st.

....
....
....
....
....

Further experiments with 80-ton gnr.

Salmon fishing commences about
this time.

FEBRUARY 2nd.

. . . .

. . . .

. . . .

. . . .

FEBRUARY 3rd.

. . . .

. . . .

. . . .

. . . .

Women's Suffrage Meeting,
Manchester, 1880.

FEBRUARY 4th.

. . . .

. . . .

. . . .

. . . .

Fair on the Thames, 1814.

Midhat Pasha expelled from Turkey, 1878.

FEBRUARY 5th.

....
....
....
....
....
....

FEBRUARY 6th.

....
....
....
....

Fox-hunting still goes on.

FEBRUARY 7th.

....
....
....
....

Sun rises, 7.32 a.m.

Russo-Turkish treaty signed, 1879.

FEBRUARY 8th.

....

....

....

....

....

FEBRUARY 9th.

....

....

....

....

....

Zulu war commenced about this time, 1879.

FEBRUARY 10th.

....

....

....

....

Reinforcements for the Cape, 1881.

FEBRUARY 11th.

Several poultry shows take place
about now.

FEBRUARY 12th.

Tops are in.

FEBRUARY 13th.

The Eve of St. Valentine.

FEBRUARY 14th.

....
....
....
....
....

St. Valentine's Day.

FEBRUARY 15th.

....
....
....
....
....

Partridges now pair.

FEBRUARY 16th.

....
....
....
....

Coursing Days.

Attempt to blow up the Emperor
of Russia.

FEBRUARY 17th.

....

....

....

....

....

FEBRUARY 18th.

....

....

....

....

....

Walking match at the Agricultural
Hall, 1880.

Zulu war continues, 1879.

FEBRUARY 19th.

....

....

....

....

Sow now.

FEBRUARY 20th.

. . . .

. . . .

. . . .

. . . .

FEBRUARY 21st.

. . . .

. . . .

. . . .

. . . .

Pancake-day about now.

FEBRUARY 22nd.

. . . .

. . . .

. . . .

. . . .

George Washington cutting his
father's tree on his sixth birthday.

Football times.

FEBRUARY 23rd.

....

....

....

....

FEBRUARY 24th.

....

....

....

....

Cart-horse show at the Agricultural
Hall, 1881.

FEBRUARY 25th.

....

....

....

....

Old Masters still at the Royal
Academy.

Sweep your door Marm.

FEBRUARY 26th.

....

....

....

....

....

FEBRUARY 27th.

....

....

....

....

....

Muffins.

Supplies sent to the Cape.

FEBRUARY 28th.

....

....

....

....

....

Hare-hunting ends

FEBRUARY 29th.

....

....

....

....

MARCH 1st.

....

....

....

....

March winds now commence to blow,

And continue until the end of the
month.

MARCH 2nd.

....

....

....

....

Boys should now fly their kites.

MARCH 3rd.

. . . .

. . . .

. . . .

. . . .

. . . .

MARCH 4th.

. . . .

. . . .

. . . .

. . . .

Hares are now mad.

Gardens should now be carefully
attended.

MARCH 5th.

. . . .

. . . .

. . . .

Execution of Guy Faux, 1606.

MARCH 6th.

MARCH 7th.

Rooks build.

MARCH 8th.

Riots at New Orleans, 1873.

MARCH 9th.

....

....

....

....

Still Fox-hunt.

MARCH 10th.

....

....

....

....

Tulips now in flower.

MARCH 11th.

....

....

....

....

First London daily paper issued, 1702.

Paper-chasing begins.

MARCH 12th.

....

....

....

....

MARCH 13th.

....

....

....

....

....

Hares are still mad.

Early chickens should be carefully
attended to.

MARCH 14th.

....

....

....

....

Indian newspapers suppressed, 1880.

MARCH 15th.

....

....

....

....

MARCH 16th.

....

....

....

....

....

West Somerset Steeplechases.

St. Patrick's Day

MARCH 17th.

....

....

....

....

Riots in Belfast about this time, 1880.

MARCH 18th.

....

....

....

....

MARCH 19th.

....

....

....

....

....

Great Earthquake in South
America, 1873.

Lambs gambol now.

MARCH 20th.

....

....

....

....

....

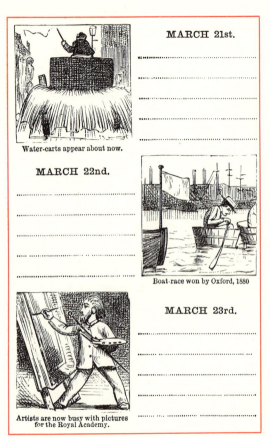

Water-carts appear about now.

MARCH 21st.

....
....
....
....
....

MARCH 22nd.

....
....
....
....
....

Boat-race won by Oxford, 1880.

MARCH 23rd.

....
....
....
....
....

Artists are now busy with pictures
for the Royal Academy.

MARCH 24th.

Hurricane in England, 1880.

MARCH 25th.

Rents are now due to Landlords.

MARCH 26th.

Kites fly now.

Sun rises, 5.40.

MARCH 27th.

....
....
....
....

MARCH 28th.

....
....
....
....

Sending in pictures to the Royal
Academy.

MARCH 29th.

....
....
....
....

Volunteer Review, at Brighton, 1880.

Expedition to North Pole, 1818.

MARCH 30th.

MARCH 31st.

Bromley Race Meeting.

APRIL 1st.

All Fools' Day.

Commencement of April showers.

APRIL 2nd.

....
....
....
....
....

APRIL 3rd.

....
....
....
....
....

Lay in stock of umbrellas for April.

APRIL 4th.

....
....
....
....

Game licences expire.

Common lodging-houses to be white-washed this week.

APRIL 5th.

APRIL 6th.

Old Lady-day.

Cats-meat-man still goes his rounds.

APRIL 7th.

Village Fairs begin.

APRIL 8th.

....
....
....
....
....

APRIL 9th.

....
....
....
....
....

Trout fishing in the Thames goes on.

APRIL 10th.

....
....
....
....
....

Young rabbits now appear.

Prepare cricket grounds now.

APRIL 11th.

APRIL 12th.

America discovered, 1492.

APRIL 13th.

Abyssinian war ended, 1868.

APRIL 14th.

April showers.

APRIL 15th.

Sun rises, 5 hrs. 6 min.

APRIL 16th.

Ornaments for your firestoves.

APRIL 17th.

Cuckoo is heard.

APRIL 18th.

Bank Holiday, 1881.

APRIL 19th.

Cricket commences about now.

Battle between British and Afghans, 1880.

APRIL 20th.

....

....

....

....

....

APRIL 21st.

....

....

....

....

....

Great fire in Canada, 1880.

Pick primroses now.

APRIL 22nd.

....

....

....

....

....

Shakespeare Festival, Stratford-on-Avon, 1879.

APRIL 23rd.

....
....
....
....

APRIL 24th.

....
....
....
....

Several Racing Meetings now.

Hot Cross Buns.

APRIL 25th.

....
....
....
....

Robinson Crusoe makes a ladder,
1659.

APRIL 26th.

....

....

....

....

APRIL 27th.

....

....

....

....

Varnishing day at the Royal Academy
about now.

APRIL 28th.

....

....

....

....

Great bicycle race at the Agricultural
Hall commenced, 1879.

Shock of earthquake felt at Doncaster, 1873.

APRIL 29th.

....

....

....

....

....

APRIL 30th.

....

....

....

....

....

Bicycle race at the Agricultural Hall continues, 1879,

MAY 1st.

....

....

....

....

....

Hail Smiling May.

Royal Academy Exhibition opens about now.

MAY 2nd.

MAY 3rd.

Trout fishing commences about now

MAY 4th.

Eggs are now plentiful.

MAY 5th.

....
....
....
....
....

Sun sets, 7.27.

MAY 6th.

....
....
....
....
....

Artists now begin to paint out of doors.

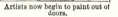

MAY 7th.

....
....
....
....

Care should be taken to keep cats from chickens.

Battle-door and shuttle-cock days.

MAY 8th.

MAY 9th.

Birds nesting looks up.

MAY 10th.

11,000 Russians banished to Siberia,
1879.

Fly catcher appears about now.

MAY 11th.

....
....
....
....
....

MAY 12th.

....
....
....
....

Relations at the Zoo.

MAY 13th.

....
....
....
....

Ice creams now become general.

Doing the Royal Academy.

MAY 14th.

....

....

....

....

....

MAY 15th.

....

....

....

....

Attempt to blow up Leeds County Court, 1879.

Fox-hounds are now idle.

MAY 16th.

....

....

....

....

A very *bowled* man.

MAY 17th.

....

....

....

....

....

MAY 18th.

....

....

....

....

Robinson Crusoe settles down in the Island, 1660.

Young ducks take possession of the Thames.

MAY 19th.

....

....

....

....

....

Young rabbits come out for romps.

MAY 20th.

....
....
....
....
....

MAY 21st.

....
....
....
....
....

Boating now commences.

Many swallows make a summer

MAY 22nd.

....
....
....
....
....

Grass fields now laid up for
mowing.

MAY 23rd.

....
....
....
....
....

MAY 24th.

....
....
....
....

May is in blossom about now.

Fenian raid on Canada, 1870.

MAY 25th.

....
....
....
....

Derby won by " Bend Or," 1880.

MAY 26th.

....

....

....

....

....

MAY 27th.

....

....

....

....

....

Great storm in Lancashire, 1878.

April showers have brought May
flowers.

MAY 28th.

....

....

....

....

Oak-apple Day.

MAY 29th.

MAY 30th.

Oaks won by "Wheel of Fortune,"
1879.

MAY 31st.

Horse show at the Agricultural Hall,
1879.

JUNE 1st.

....

....

....

....

....

Royal Academy still open

JUNE 2nd.

....

....

....

....

....

Getting round a b(u)oy

JUNE 3rd.

....

....

....

....

....

Destructive thunderstorm in the
Midland Counties, 1879.

Hard hitting sets in.

JUNE 4th.

....

....

....

....

JUNE 5th.

....

....

....

....

....

Geraniums are now in bloom.

JUNE 6th.

....

....

....

....

....

Young birds appear about now.

JUNE 7th.

....
....
....
....
....

Great Reform Bill passed, 1832.

JUNE 8th.

....
....
....
....

Trout fishing continues.

JUNE 9th.

....
....
....
....

Haymaking commences about now.

Great sails at this time.

JUNE 10th.

....

....

....

....

JUNE 11th.

....

....

....

....

....

Snuff-taking originated in Ireland, 1565.

Leap-frog established 98710.

JUNE 12th.

....

....

....

....

All a-blowing, all a-growing.

JUNE 13th.

....
....
....
....
....

JUNE 14th.

....
....
....
....
....

International Rifle match, 1880.

JUNE 15th.

....
....
....
....

Haymaking slowly carried on.

JUNE 16th.

Sculling match on the Tyne, 1879.

JUNE 17th.

Rabbits may now have green food.

The Order of the Bath.

JUNE 18th.

JUNE 19th.

Horse show at the Alexandra Palace, 1878.

JUNE 20th.

Sun rises, 3.44.

JUNE 21st.

Sun sets 8.18, longest day.

Russians cross the Danube, 1877.

JUNE 22nd.

....

....

....

....

....

JUNE 23rd.

....

....

....

....

....

Great fire in Tooley Street, 1861.

Thermometer too many in the shade.

JUNE 24th.

....

....

....

....

....

South Kensington Museum opened, 1855.

JUNE 25th.

JUNE 26th.

Folks go sailing and come back ailing.

JUNE 27th.

Good many balls at this season.

Koh-i-noor diamond arrived in
England, 1850.

JUNE 28th.

....

....

....

....

....

JUNE 29th.

....

....

....

....

Earthquake in Venetia, 1873.

Reception of Foreign Ambassadors
by the Emperor of China.

JUNE 30th.

....

....

....

....

JULY 1st.

Dog-days commence.

JULY 2nd.

Discovery of a Comet, 1873.

JULY 3rd.

The day before the battle of Ulundi, 1879.

Festival of American Independence.

JULY 4th.

....

....

....

....

JULY 5th.

....

....

....

....

....

Royal Agricultural Society's Show,
Kilburn, 1879.

Dog-days continue.

JULY 6th.

....

....

....

....

....

JULY 7th.

A few days after the battle of Ulundi, 1879.

JULY 8th.

Bull-rush in flower now.

JULY 9th.

Great earthquake in Valparaiso, 1873.

Lawn Tennis breaks out.

JULY 10th.

....

....

....

....

....

JULY 11th.

....

....

....

....

....

Fighting in Crete and Bosnia, 1878.

Crimea Evacuated, 1856.

JULY 12th.

....

....

....

....

Flight of Cetewayo, 1879.

JULY 13th.

JULY 14th.

British Flag hoisted at Cyprus, 1878.

JULY 15th.

St. Swithin's Day.

Intense heat in England, 1868.

JULY 16th.

....
....
....
....
....

JULY 17th.

....
....
....
....
....

Pic-nic now.

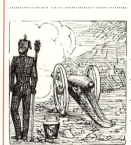

Attack on the Shipka Pass, 1877.

JULY 18th.

....
....
....
....
....

Sun sets, 8.5.

JULY 19th.

....

....

....

....

JULY 20th.

....

....

....

....

....

Spanish Armada defeated, 1588

Yachting sets in severely.

JULY 21st.

....

....

....

....

....

Presentation of testimonial to
W. G. Grace, the eminent cricketer.

JULY 22nd.

....
....
....
....
....
....

JULY 23rd.

....
....
....
....
....

Insurrection in Dublin, 1803.

JULY 24th.

....
....
....
....
....

Sun-flower now in bloom.

Artists still paint out of doors.

JULY 25th.

....

....

....

....

....

JULY 26th.

....

....

....

....

....

Bombardment of Cadiz by
Insurgents, 1873.

Atlantic Cable laid, 1866.

JULY 27th.

....

....

....

....

Ramadan, month of abstinence
observed by the Turks com.

JULY 28th.

....
....
....
....
....
....

JULY 29th.

....
....
....
....
....

"Alabama" sailed from the
Mersey, 1862.

JULY 30th.

....
....
....
....
....

Mine explosion, 1864.

St. Helena discovered, 1502.

JULY 31st.

....

....

....

....

....

AUGUST 1st.

....

....

....

....

....

Bank Holiday about now.

Royal Yachting Society's Regatta,
1880.

AUGUST 2nd.

....

....

....

....

Pursuit of Cetewayo commenced, 1879.

AUGUST 3rd.

....

....

....

....

....

AUGUST 4th.

....

....

....

....

Go to the seaside now.

Iquique bombarded by the Chilean Fleet, 1879.

AUGUST 5th.

....

....

....

....

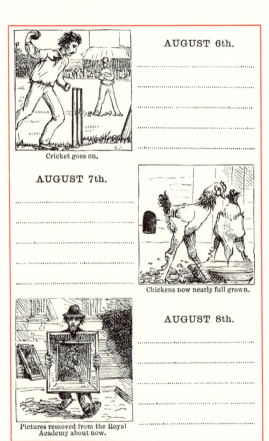

Cricket goes on.

AUGUST 6th.

....
....
....
....
....

AUGUST 7th.

....
....
....
....
....

Chickens now nearly full grown.

AUGUST 8th.

....
....
....
....
....

Pictures removed from the Royal
Academy about now.

Izaac Walton born, 1593.

AUGUST 9th.

....

....

....

....

....

AUGUST 10th.

....

....

....

....

....

Robbery of arms at Cork, 1880.

Dog days end.

AUGUST 11th.

....

....

....

....

Grouse shooting begins.

AUGUST 12th.

....
....
....
....
....

AUGUST 13th.

....
....
....
....
....

Sun sets, 7.2

Harvesting commences about now

AUGUST 14th.

....
....
....
....

Fatal riots at Lurgan, 1879.

AUGUST 15th.

··

··

··

··

··

AUGUST 16th.

··

··

··

··

··

Apples are good now.

Great comet, 1682.

AUGUST 17th.

··

··

··

··

··

Outbreak of Holidays at the
seaside.

AUGUST 18th.

....

....

....

....

AUGUST 19th.

....

....

....

....

Gas first used in London, 1807.

Bombardment of Omao by one of
Her Majesty's ships, 1873.

AUGUST 20th.

....

....

....

Blackcock shooting commences.

AUGUST 21st.

....

....

....

....

AUGUST 22nd.

....

....

....

....

"Fine apples! three a penny!"

AUGUST 23rd.

....

....

....

....

Boats are "in" still.

Fearful gales off Nova Scotia, 1873.

AUGUST 24th

....

....

....

....

....

AUGUST 25th.

....

....

....

....

....

Grouse shooting continues.

Opening of the Birmingham Musical
Festival, 1879.

AUGUST 26th.

....

....

....

....

Nuts are now ripe.

AUGUST 27th.

....
....
....
....
....

AUGUST 28th.

....
....
....
....
....

Sun rises at 5.7.

Terrific hurricane at Bermuda
Islands, 1880.

AUGUST 29th.

....
....
....
....
....

Eruption of Mount Etna, 1874.

AUGUST 30th.

....

....

....

....

....

AUGUST 31st.

....

....

....

....

....

Harvesting continues.

Partridge shooting commences.

SEPTEMBER 1st.

....

....

....

....

....

Coronation of Cetewayo as King of
the Zulus, 1873.

SEPTEMBER 2nd.

....

....

....

....

SEPTEMBER 3rd.

....

....

....

....

London burnt, 1666.

Sun rises, 5.19.

SEPTEMBER 4th.

....

....

....

....

Drawing the long bow.

SEPTEMBER 5th.

....

....

....

....

....

SEPTEMBER 6th.

....

....

....

....

....

Cricket match, England v. Australia
commenced, 1880.

SEPTEMBER 7th.

....

....

....

....

Balloons continually sent from
Paris, 1870.

Mushrooms spring up.

SEPTEMBER 8th.

....

....

....

....

....

SEPTEMBER 9th.

....

....

....

....

Trout fishing ends.

SEPTEMBER 10th.

....

....

....

....

Cricket ends about now.

Opening of Brighton Free Museum
and Picture Gallery, 1873.

SEPTEMBER 11th.

....

....

....

....

SEPTEMBER 12th.

....

....

....

....

Cleopatra's Needle erected in
London, 1878.

SEPTEMBER 13th.

....

....

....

....

Harvest of the poor.

Apples fall about now.

SEPTEMBER 14th.

....

....

....

....

SEPTEMBER 15th.

....

....

....

....

Doncaster races, 1880.

SEPTEMBER 16th.

....

....

....

....

Lawn Tennis in full bloom.

International Potato Show, Crystal Palace, 1879.

SEPTEMBER 17th.

....

....

....

....

....

SEPTEMBER 18th.

....

....

....

....

Heavy fall in pears.

Worcester fair.

SEPTEMBER 19th.

....

....

....

....

Battle of Alma, 1854.

SEPTEMBER 20th.

....
....
....
....
....

SEPTEMBER 21st.

....
....
....
....
....

100 days to the end of the year.

SEPTEMBER 22nd.

....
....
....
....
....

Partridge shooting commences in
Ireland.

SEPTEMBER 23rd.

Autumn begins.

SEPTEMBER 24th.

Sun sets, 5.54.

Siege of Paris commenced, 1870.

SEPTEMBER 25th.

Electric telegraph commenced, 1851.

SEPTEMBER 26th.

....

....

....

....

....

SEPTEMBER 27th.

....

....

....

....

....

First railway opened, Stockton and
Darlington, 1825.

SEPTEMBER 28th.

....

....

....

....

Michaelmas geese.

SEPTEMBER 29th.

Birmingham Onion Fair about now.

SEPTEMBER 30th.

Coals first brought to London, 1357.

OCTOBER 1st.

Pheasant shooting commences.

This is the best month for brewing ales.

OCTOBER 2nd.

....

....

....

....

....

OCTOBER 3rd.

....

....

....

....

....

Dublin first lighted with gas, 1825.

OCTOBER 4th.

....

....

....

....

Foot-ball begins about now.

Yankee Doodling it.

OCTOBER 5th.

....
....
....
....

OCTOBER 6th.

....
....
....
....

Robinson Crusoe discovered foot-
prints on the sand, 1660.

OCTOBER 7th.

....
....
....
....

Hurricane, Calcutta, 1864.

Fire in Chicago, 1871.

OCTOBER 8th.

....

....

....

....

....

OCTOBER 9th.

....

....

....

....

Nuts are to be gathered in.

Great Fair, Weyhill, and 5 following days

OCTOBER 10th.

....

....

....

....

Order of the Bath instituted, 1399.

OCTOBER 11th.

....
....
....
....
....

OCTOBER 12th.

....
....
....
....
....

Eighty days to the end of the year.

Robinson Crusoe carried goods from
ship to the island, 1659.

OCTOBER 13th.

....
....
....
....
....

Leaves begin to fall about now.

OCTOBER 14th.

....
....
....
....
....

OCTOBER 15th.

....
....
....
....
....

Inundation of St. Petersburg, 1873.

OCTOBER 16th.

....
....
....
....

Great floods in Spain, 1879.

Leaf-taking.

OCTOBER 17th.

....
....
....
....

OCTOBER 18th.

....
....
....
....

Melbourne International Exhibition
now open, 1880.

OCTOBER 19th.

....
....
....
....

Rope walking on board the
"Poonah," by M. Blondin.

Wild duck shooting continues.

OCTOBER 20th.

....

....

....

....

OCTOBER 21st.

....

....

....

....

....

Battle of Trafalgar, 1805.

Hare and hounds.

OCTOBER 22nd.

....

....

....

....

....

Cub hunting begins about now.

OCTOBER 23rd.

....

....

....

....

....

OCTOBER 24th.

....

....

....

....

....

Cartes de Visite first taken at Nice, 1857.

OCTOBER 25th.

....

....

....

....

Saint Crispin.

The 300th day of the year.

OCTOBER 26th.

....

....

....

....

....

OCTOBER 27th.

....

....

....

....

....

124th day of Tichborne trial in Court
of Queen's Bench, 1873.

OCTOBER 28th.

....

....

....

....

....

Bank Acts suspended, 1849.

OCTOBER 29th.

Riots at Bristol, 1831.

OCTOBER 30th.

Hare hunting begins about now.

OCTOBER 31st.

Chill October.

Dedication of new bells at St. Paul's
1878.

NOVEMBER 1st.

....

....

....

....

NOVEMBER 2nd.

....

....

....

....

November fogs begin.

Hare hunting continues.

NOVEMBER 3rd.

....

....

....

....

....

Explosion at a fire-work makers,
Lambeth, 1873.

NOVEMBER 4th.

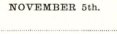

NOVEMBER 5th.

Gunpowder Plot discovered, 1605.

New York Festivities about now.

NOVEMBER 6th.

Rabbiting.

NOVEMBER 7th.

....

....

....

....

NOVEMBER 8th.

....

....

....

....

Fox-hunting continues.

NOVEMBER 9th.

....

....

....

....

Lord Mayor's day.

Wild geese return about now.

NOVEMBER 10th.

....

....

....

....

....

NOVEMBER 11th.

....

....

....

....

....

Wood-pigeon shooting.

NOVEMBER 12th.

Average temperature for this day.

....

....

....

....

....

Fox-hunting.

NOVEMBER 13th.

....

....

....

....

....

NOVEMBER 14th.

....

....

....

....

....

Snow must now be expected.

Foot-ball continues.

NOVEMBER 15th.

....

....

....

....

....

National Volunteer Association
established, 1859.

NOVEMBER 16th.

....

....

....

....

NOVEMBER 17th.

....

....

....

....

....

Last convict landed in Sydney, 1840.

First balloon ascended, 1782.

NOVEMBER 18th.

....

....

....

....

Sun Sets, 4.4.

NOVEMBER 19th.

....

....

....

....

....

NOVEMBER 20th.

....

....

....

....

....

A dark look out.

NOVEMBER 21st.

....

....

....

....

....

Fox-hunting continues.

Winter fuel.

NOVEMBER 22nd.

....

....

....

....

NOVEMBER 23rd.

....

....

....

....

Sun rises 7.34.

The opening of Thames Southern
Embankment, 1869.

NOVEMBER 24th.

....

....

....

....

In for a good thing.

NOVEMBER 25th.

....

....

....

....

....

NOVEMBER 26th.

....

....

....

.. . .

....

Rabbiting still goes on.

NOVEMBER 27th.

... .

....

....

....

....

Eddystone Light-house destroyed,
1703.

Great fall in corduroys.

NOVEMBER 28th.

....

....

....

....

NOVEMBER 29th.

....

....

....

....

....

First London School Board, 1879.

Sun sets 3.53.

NOVEMBER 30th.

....

....

....

....

....

Making a pile.

DECEMBER 1st.

....

....

....

....

DECEMBER 2nd.

....

....

....

....

"Sweep your door, Marm."

Slippery proceedings.

DECEMBER 3rd.

....

....

....

....

A (n) ice meeting.

DECEMBER 4th.

....

....

....

....

DECEMBER 5th.

....

....

....

....

Out pensioners.

" We've got no work to do-oo."

DECEMBER 6th.

....

....

....

....

Fox-hunting goes on, weather permitting.

DECEMBER 7th.

....
....
....
....
....

DECEMBER 8th.

....
....
....
....
....

Twenty-three days to the end of the year.

Sleighing continues.

DECEMBER 9th.

....
....
....
....
....

Black game and grouse shooting ends.

DECEMBER 10th.

....
....
....
....
....

DECEMBER 11th.

....
....
....
....
....

Bringing home the holly.

DECEMBER 12th.

....
....
....
....
....

A square fall.

First Smithfield Cattle Show, 1799.

DECEMBER 13th.

....

....

....

....

....

DECEMBER 14th.

....

....

....

....

....

Goloshes in demand.

Gun cotton invented, 1845.

DECEMBER 15th.

....

....

....

....

....

Christmas holidays commence
about now.

DECEMBER 16th.

....

....

....

....

DECEMBER 17th.

....

....

....

....

Store up provisions for Christmas.

Bronze coin issued, 1860.

DECEMBER 18th.

....

....

....

....

Christmas trees.

DECEMBER 19th.

....

....

....

....

DECEMBER 20th

....

....

....

....

More Christmas trees.

DECEMBER 21st.

....

....

....

....

Shortest day, sun sets 3.51.

Christmas visitors.

DECEMBER 22nd.

....
....
....
....
....

DECEMBER 23rd

....
....
....
....

More Christmas visitors.

DECEMBER 24th.

....
....
....
....

The waits.

Christmas Day.

DECEMBER 25th.

....
....
....
....
....
....

DECEMBER 26th.

....
....
....
....

Boxing Day.

Average daily temperature 37°.

DECEMBER 27th.

....
....
....
....
....

Great snow-storm in Scotland, 1878.

DECEMBER 28th.

....

....

....

....

....

DECEMBER 29th.

....

....

....

....

Provide physic for children after
festivities.

DECEMBER 30th.

....

....

....

....

....

The Mistletoe Bough.

DECEMBER 31st.

....

....

....

....

Last day of the year.

THE END of MY DIARY.